In a world of rapid technological and mechanical advancements, humanity expanded forests into cities. They achieved artificial plants, synthetic food, and even created artificial pets. As a result, plants and animals became obsolete to humans. At this point, humans believed they could completely detach from natural existence.

As human civilization thrived, forests are disappearing, and animals migrated towards a particular location. Then, 14 years ago, all animals mysteriously vanished within the last remaining forest, the only one left. This forest's survival is due to a mysterious energy that renders modern human tools ineffective and people get lost in it, thus humans stop entering the forest. The forest is named the "Last Forest" since then.

In a busy city with towering buildings, some people grew tired. They built a quiet village near the "Last Forest". It felt old-fashioned compared to the bustling city, but people lived happily there.

Megan is a cheerful 14-year-old girl who is kind and caring. She lives in a village near the "Last Forest", spreading love and positivity wherever she goes.

One night, as Megan was getting ready for bed,
she discovered a fox in her room. The fox hopped
onto her bed, surprising Megan. He was the first
real fox she had ever seen, as all the animals had
vanished long ago. However, the most amazing
thing was that the fox could communicate his
thoughts to Megan. He told her that he had gotten
lost while playing and needed help finding his way
home.

After hearing the fox's thoughts, Megan
enthusiastically wanted to help. She hurried to
her study and started researching. She
remembered her elders saying that all the animals
vanished in the "Last Forest", so the clues must
lie there. Then she searched for information about
that forest and found a map.

On the map, there was a small cabin deep in the forest. Looking at it, Megan remembered something strange her elders mentioned before. Some people claimed to have seen the cabin at the marked spot, while others said there was nothing there. But even those who saw it didn't know what was inside because no one could get in. Megan thought the cabin might be connected to the missing animals and decided to explore it the next day.

The next morning, with the sky still dim, Megan and the fox headed to the "Last Forest". Once inside, Megan knew that all human devices would stop working, so she came prepared with candles to light their path as they ventured deeper into the forest.

Time passed quickly, and the sun was about to set. Finally, Megan and the fox reached the spot marked on the map. Just as Megan had hoped, she spotted a little cabin with lights shining. It seemed like someone lived there. Curious, she decided to knock on the door.

Megan knocked on the door, but there was no answer. She gently pulled the door, and it swung open, revealing a dazzling light. As the light dimmed, Megan was amazed by the sight before her.

The door led to another realm, a world completely
different from the outside. Megan found herself
in a magical and enchanting forest, filled with tall
and lush trees, diverse plants, sparkling lights and
a wide variety of animals - flying in the sky,
walking on land, and swimming in the water, all
living freely.

Upon entering, a deer welcomed them. Megan realized the deer could communicate with her too. The deer thanked Megan for bringing the fox back to the forest and explained that all the animals here had evolved intelligence and could communicate through thoughts. She guided Megan on a path and then allowed Megan to freely explore the magical surroundings.

Megan met a friendly elephant. The elephant greeted her warmly and shared that he had been 14 years since he last saw a human. It reminisced about the happy moments he had shared with some humans. Despite losing his habitat due to human development, the elephant harbored no ill will. He simply hoped for a chance to return to the original world once again.

After talking to the elephant, Megan encountered a giraffe. The giraffe was also delighted to see a human again. She shared a story about how a kind-hearted human helped treat her mother's leg injury 15 years ago, enabling her mother to walk again. She expressed gratitude towards humans. Although the forest was beautiful, she still missed the old world. Moved by the elephant and giraffe's stories, Megan felt a strong desire to help the animals return to their original world.

As Megan pondered the animals' plight, she spotted two large foxes emerging from deep within the forest. They were the parents of the fox, coming to take their child home. They expressed immense gratitude to Megan for returning their little one safely.

As the time came to say goodbye, Megan and the fox bid farewell with sadness. Megan was delighted to see him reunited with his family. The fox expressed gratitude to Megan and hoped to meet her again someday.

Watching the fox and his family leave, Megan felt a twinge of sadness. However, seeing their happy and content expressions, she knew it was all worth it. She wondered if the animals could return to their original world, would she and the fox meet again?

After the fox left, Megan began exploring the forest on her own. As she walked, countless glowing dots appeared, leading her somewhere. Following them, Megan arrived at a cave and ventured deep inside.

At the end of the cave, Megan was amazed to see a huge and incredibly beautiful phoenix. It was covered in golden feathers shining brightly, looking elegant and magnificent. Megan couldn't believe it was real because she had always been told that the phoenix was just a fictional creature in books and movies.

The phoenix introduced herself as the creator and guardian of the forest. As humans expanded cities, animals lost their habitats. Thus, she used her creative powers to craft this other-dimensional forest. 14 years ago, she gathered all animals here. The forest is full of energy, which sustains the animals, so they can live in harmony without needing to eat. The entrance to this forest is the cabin, but only those with a pure and kind heart can see it, and only animals are allowed to enter.

However, some animals held grudges against humans for taking their homes. They formed a group and are planning to return to the original world and reclaim their habitats with force. The fox may have accidentally entered the human world through a portal they created. The phoenix explained she couldn't interfere but believed Megan might change the impending tragedy.

After talking to the phoenix, Megan felt confused and worried. She thought about how to end the animals' hatred towards humans and let them return peacefully to the original world. With these thoughts, she reached the cave's entrance, but what she saw there startled her.

In front of Megan, a huge tiger appeared in the jungle across the cave. He had pale yellow stripes on his face and a mostly white body. The tiger looked fierce, roaring as if he would pounce on her any moment. Megan felt she was in extreme danger, and her heart was filled with fear.

Just as Megan was terrified, the deer that had guided her before stepped in front of her, facing the tiger. The deer told the tiger that Megan was not a bad person; she helped the fox get homemade amends for the mistake made by the tiger's group. It was they who opened the portal and caused the little fox to get lost in the human world.

Megan bravely approached the tiger and urged them to avoid violence, as it would only lead to more hatred and suffering. She didn't want anyone to get hurt. She also reminded them of the advanced weapons humans possessed, making it a losing battle for the animals. Then she proposed a peaceful solution to let the animals return to their world.

Megan told them she found countless purple ores in the forest, which humans don't have. It could be valuable to humans. If the ores were just regular stones in this forest, they could trade with humans to rebuild their homes. The tiger calmed down and agreed to give it a try as Megan suggested.

Megan brought a few purple ores back to the village and found her dad's friend, who used to work at the national research institute and had scientific equipment at home. Megan hoped he could help examine the ores. She also shared her adventures in the forest and the animals' needs with him.

The researcher discovered that the purple ore was incredibly hard yet lightweight. It had the potential to significantly improve human productivity and quality in various fields, such as transportation and construction. He took the ore to the relevant authorities and explained the situation, including the animals' desire to trade with humans.

Humans agreed to the trade, and in two years, they used the purple ores to build a huge forest on the ocean, which could expand as needed. Many animals moved from the other-dimensional forest to the human-made one, and some chose not to move. From then on, all animals could freely travel between the two worlds without any obstacles.

In the new forest, some carnivores needed meat as
they no longer received Phoenix energy. Thus,
humans sent flying cargo ships with artificial meat
regularly. Now all animals lived together
harmoniously without hunting.

After the forest was built, the animals agreed to friendly interactions with humans, who could freely visit. Even the tiger put aside his grudge and often played with human kids. At the same time, humans realized artificial animals couldn't replace the real ones, especially their intelligence and emotions. Now, they lived together harmoniously.

On a sunny morning, Megan was leisurely sipping her coffee by the window, reminiscing about her adventures with the fox. She learned that the fox family chose to stay in the other-dimensional forest, and she might not see them again, which made her a bit sad. As she pondered, she suddenly heard a knock on the door.

When Megan opened the door to check, she was pleasantly surprised to find the fox standing at her doorstep. Then they smiled at each other.

The End

Author's Message:
I hope that through this story, we can realize the importance of coexistence between humans, nature, and animals. May humans and nature thrive together, creating a beautiful future. May every child become a partner in protecting animals and our precious environment.

Made in the USA
Middletown, DE
12 November 2023

42549887R00020